D0908871

THE BEST BOOK OF

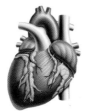

The Human Body

Barbara Taylor

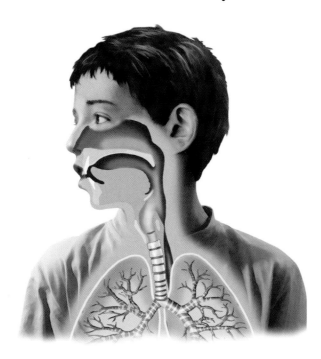

KINGFISHER
NEW YORK

Contents

KINGFISHER
Kingfisher is an imprint of Macmillan
Children's Books, London.
Published in the United States by
Kingfisher U.S., a division of Holtzbrinck
Publishing Holdings Limited Partnership,
175 Fifth Avenue, New York, New York
10010.

Distributed in Canada by H. B. Fenn
and Company Ltd.

Library of Congress Cataloging-in-
Publication Data has been applied for.

ISBN 978-0-7534-6031-3

Kingfisher books are available for special
promotions and premiums. For details
contact: Director of Special Markets,
Holtzbrinck Publishers.

First Hardback American Edition June 2008
Printed in China
10 9 8 7 6 5 4 3 2 1
1TR/1207/WKT/UNTD/128MA/C

Consultant: Dr. Patricia Macnair
Editor: Deborah Murrell
Coordinating editor: Caitlin Doyle
Art director: Mike Davis
Designer: Jack Clucas
DTP coordinator: Catherine Hibbert
Production controller: Jessamy Oldfield

All illustrations by Roger Stewart except
for pages 4 left (Mark Bergin), 6, 8 top
right, 11 top left, 13 top, 14 right, 15 left
and top, 16 right (Mark Bergin), 18
bottom right, 21 top right and bottom,
22 top right, 24 top, 25 top left, 26 top
right, 27 top left and center left, 28 left

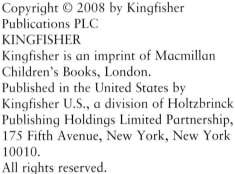

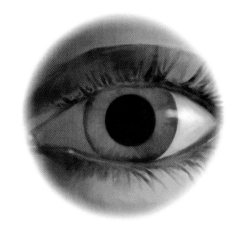

Your body

People may look very different on the outside, but they are made up of the same parts inside. Each part has its own job to do. For example, your bones and muscles help you move, and your heart pumps blood around your body. Your brain tells the different parts of your body what to do and keeps them working together so that you stay alive.

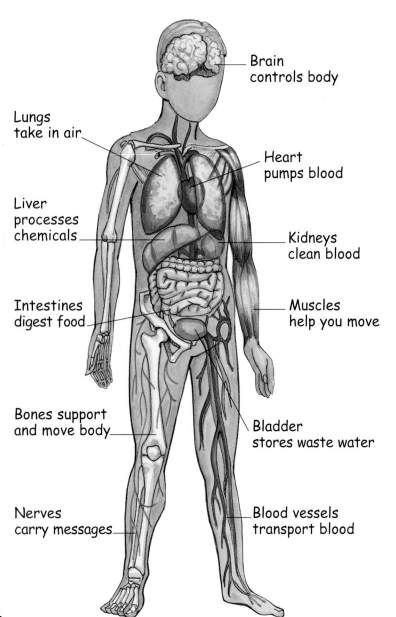

Brain
controls body

Lungs
take in air

Heart
pumps blood

Liver
processes
chemicals

Kidneys
clean blood

Intestines
digest food

Muscles
help you move

Bones support
and move body

Bladder
stores waste water

Nerves
carry messages

Blood vessels
transport blood

Inside of your body

Throughout your body there are bones, muscles, blood vessels, and nerves, which carry electrical signals. In the middle of your body there are important organs such as the heart, lungs, and kidneys.

4

Outside of your body

Your body is made up of several parts. At the top is the head. In the middle is the trunk. The top half of the trunk is called the chest, and the bottom half is called the abdomen. Your arms and legs are connected to your trunk.

You are unique

Everyone looks different—there is no one exactly like you in the entire world. Even identical twins have small differences. But family members often share similar features such as eye color.

All wrapped up

Your skin is a stretchy bag that holds your body together. It stops your body from drying out and keeps out dirt and germs. It also stops you from getting too hot or too cold and helps you feel touch, temperature, pressure, and pain. Skin contains a coloring called melanin. People with a lot of melanin have browner skin, and this protects their skin from strong sunshine, which can hurt or burn the skin.

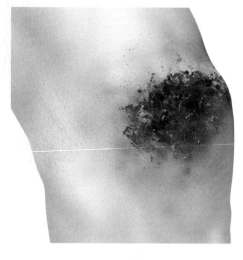

Skin repair

If you cut yourself, your blood clots and forms a scab. This scab protects the new skin that grows beneath it.

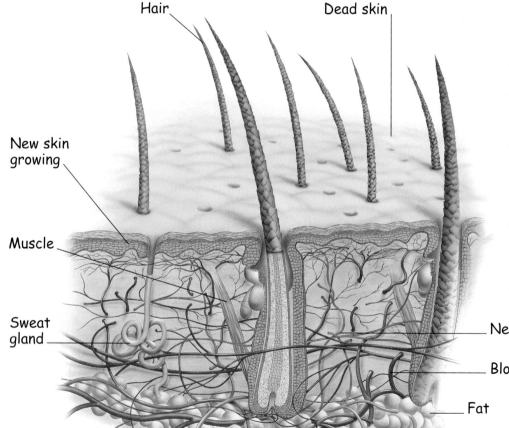

Hair

Dead skin

New skin growing

Muscle

Sweat gland

Nerve

Blood vessel

Fat

Under your skin

Your skin has several layers. The top layer is dead skin, which flakes off all the time. Below this, new skin grows. The middle layer is where hair and nails start to grow and where sweat is made. This layer has blood vessels and nerves. The bottom layer is fat.

Cooling down

When you run around and get hot, you turn red because the blood vessels in your skin get wider. More blood flows close to the surface so that the air can cool it and your body.

Hairy heads

Most of your hair is on your head. This helps protect your skin and keep you warm. Like skin, hair color depends on how much melanin it contains.

Sunblock blocks out the sun's harmful rays and protects the skin from damage.

7

Thinking and doing

Inside your head is the most important part of your body—your brain. It takes up around half of your head, and it is the part of you that thinks, remembers, and figures out new ways of doing things. Your brain also keeps the rest of your body working. It works all day and all night without you even being aware of it.

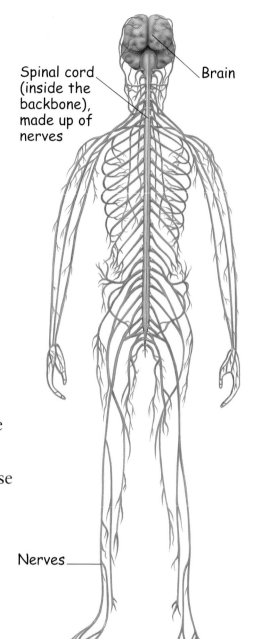

Spinal cord (inside the backbone), made up of nerves

Brain

Nerves

Computer brain

Your brain is more complex than a computer. It receives information from your senses, thinks about what to do, and sends signals to tell your muscles what to do.

Sending signals

Your brain is linked to the rest of your body by thin threads called nerves. These carry electrical signals to and from your brain.

Sleep gives your body time to grow, heal itself, and make sense of events that happened during the day.

The five senses

Your brain collects information through your senses: sight, hearing, smell, taste, and touch. From your eyes, ears, nose, tongue, and skin, your nerves send signals to your brain, which tells your body how to react.

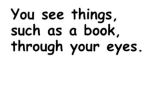

You see things, such as a book, through your eyes.

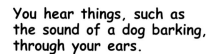

You hear things, such as the sound of a dog barking, through your ears.

You touch things, such as a spiky cactus, with your skin, which is all over your body. Your skin is your body's largest sense organ.

You taste things, such as yogurt, through your tongue.

You smell things, such as the sweet scent of flowers, through your nose.

Seeing the world

Sight is the most important of your five senses. You see an object when light bounces off it and enters your eyes. Your eyes can sense many different colors. Both eyes face forward, which helps you figure out how far away things are. This also helps you see 3-D shapes instead of just a flat world.

Pictures of your world

Your eyes work in a similar way to a camera. Light passes through a lens that gathers, or focuses, the light to produce a clear picture on the back of your eye (the retina).

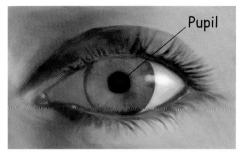

Pupil

The iris is a ring of muscle that changes the size of the pupil. In bright light the iris makes the pupil smaller to stop too much light from entering the eye.

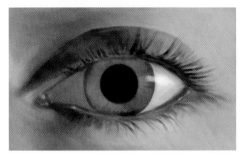

In dim light the pupil widens to let more light into the eye.

10

This picture shows what the inside of your eye looks like.

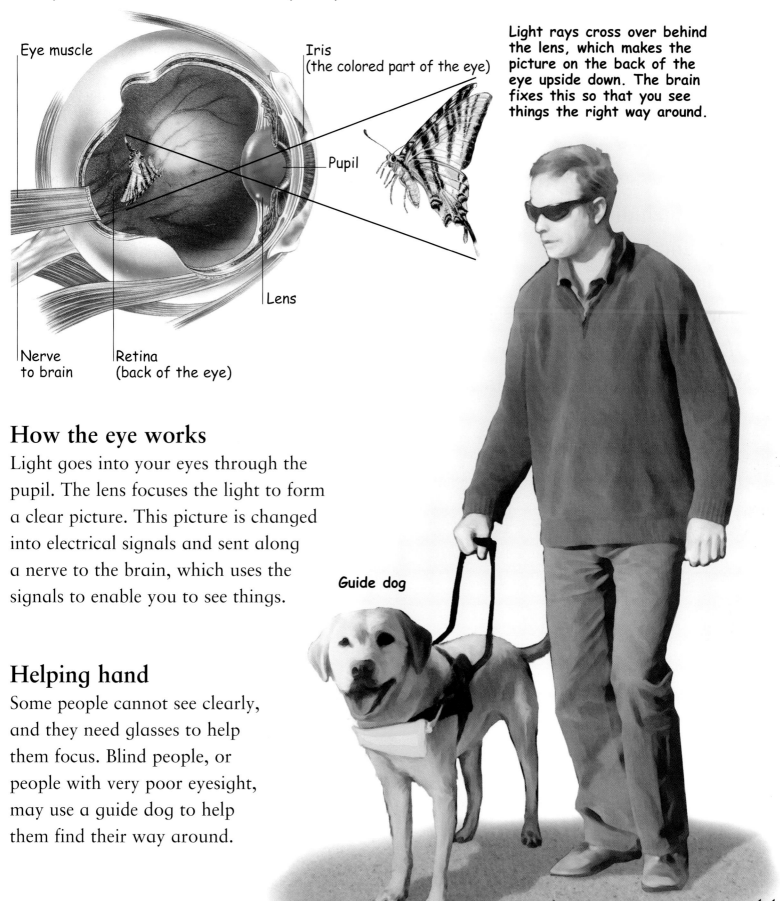

Eye muscle

Iris
(the colored part of the eye)

Pupil

Lens

Nerve to brain

Retina
(back of the eye)

Light rays cross over behind the lens, which makes the picture on the back of the eye upside down. The brain fixes this so that you see things the right way around.

How the eye works

Light goes into your eyes through the pupil. The lens focuses the light to form a clear picture. This picture is changed into electrical signals and sent along a nerve to the brain, which uses the signals to enable you to see things.

Helping hand

Some people cannot see clearly, and they need glasses to help them focus. Blind people, or people with very poor eyesight, may use a guide dog to help them find their way around.

Guide dog

11

Hearing things

Your ears pick up sounds from all around you. With one ear on each side of your head, you can tell which direction a sound is coming from. The sound will be louder in the ear that is closest to it. People who cannot hear very well may wear hearing aids in their ears to make sounds louder.

Your ears help you balance.

Balance
Inside each ear there are tubes of liquid. Nerves detect movement in the liquid and send signals to your brain that tell you where your head is and how it is moving. This makes it easier to balance.

Musical sounds
Sounds are made when something shakes back and forth very quickly (vibrates). This violin makes the air vibrate. The strings are stretched so that each one produces a different note.

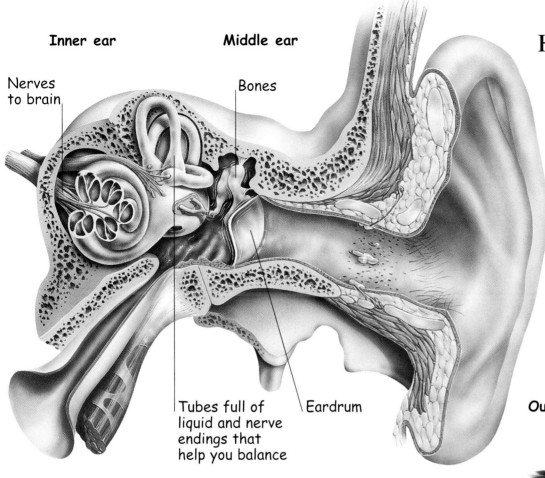

Inner ear

Middle ear

Nerves
to brain

Bones

Tubes full of
liquid and nerve
endings that
help you balance

Eardrum

Outer ear

How the ear works

The outer ear funnels
sounds into your head.
Three tiny bones in
the middle ear make the
sounds stronger and pass
them into the inner ear.
This sends signals to the
brain, which allows you
to hear the sounds.

Making sounds louder

When a person speaks
into a megaphone, the
special cone shape
stops the sound of
their voice from
spreading out. This
concentrates the sound
and makes it louder.

In your mouth

Your mouth is the place through which food enters your body. Inside of your mouth are your teeth and tongue. Your teeth cut, chew, and grind food, while your tongue rolls it into a ball and pushes it to the back of your mouth, ready to be swallowed. Your mouth is also where you make sounds such as speaking, singing, and whistling.

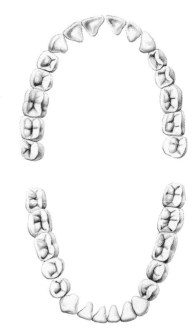

20 milk teeth are usually formed by the age of two.

Your tongue is covered with little bumps that contain tiny taste buds. These sense different tastes and send messages along nerves to your brain.

28 to 32 adult teeth are usually formed between the ages of 18 to 20.

Two sets of teeth

When you are little, you grow a set of milk teeth, or baby teeth. When your mouth gets bigger, larger teeth grow beneath your milk teeth and gradually push them all out.

Inside a tooth

Tooth enamel is the hardest substance in the body. Below this is a softer layer of dentin, which helps absorb knocks to the teeth. Inside of the dentin there are nerves and blood vessels.

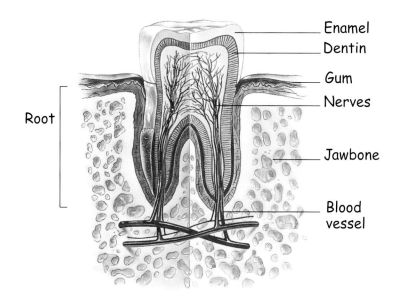

- Enamel
- Dentin
- Gum
- Nerves
- Root
- Jawbone
- Blood vessel

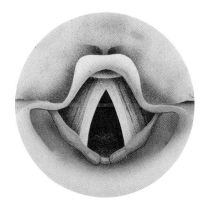

Loose, relaxed vocal cords make low-pitched sounds.

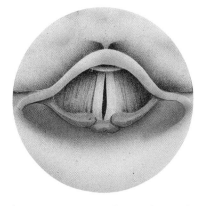

Tight, tense vocal cords make high-pitched sounds.

Sounds of speech

The sounds made by the vocal cords travel up your throat and into your mouth. You form the sounds into words by changing the shape of your tongue, your lips, and your cheeks.

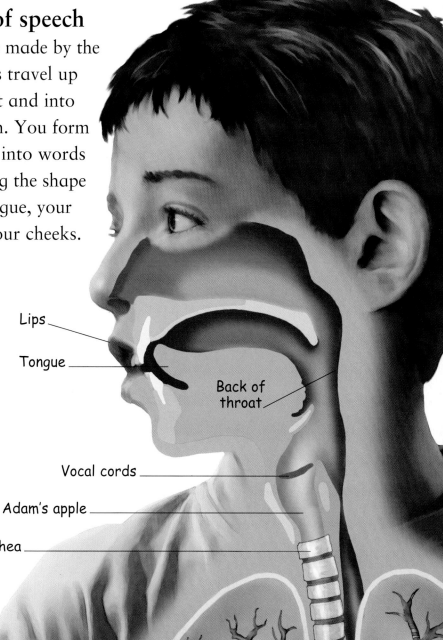

- Lips
- Tongue
- Back of throat
- Vocal cords
- Adam's apple
- Trachea

Making sounds

Two vocal cords stretch across the top of your trachea, or windpipe. As air goes through the vocal cords, it makes them wobble, or vibrate, producing sounds.

Eating food

Food gives your body the energy that it needs in order to grow and work properly. Before you can use the food you eat, it has to be broken down into smaller pieces. Then the nutrients in the food can pass into your blood and be carried around your body to where they are needed. This process of breaking down food is called digestion.

Watery body

Drinking water is essential to keep your body working. Watery wastes are turned into urine in your kidneys. The urine goes down a tube and is stored in your bladder until you go to the bathroom.

Fruit and vegetables contain a lot of vitamins.

Proteins in milk, cheese, and fish help your body repair itself.

Potatoes, pasta, and rice give you energy.

Whole-wheat bread, vegetables, beans, and nuts help your digestive system.

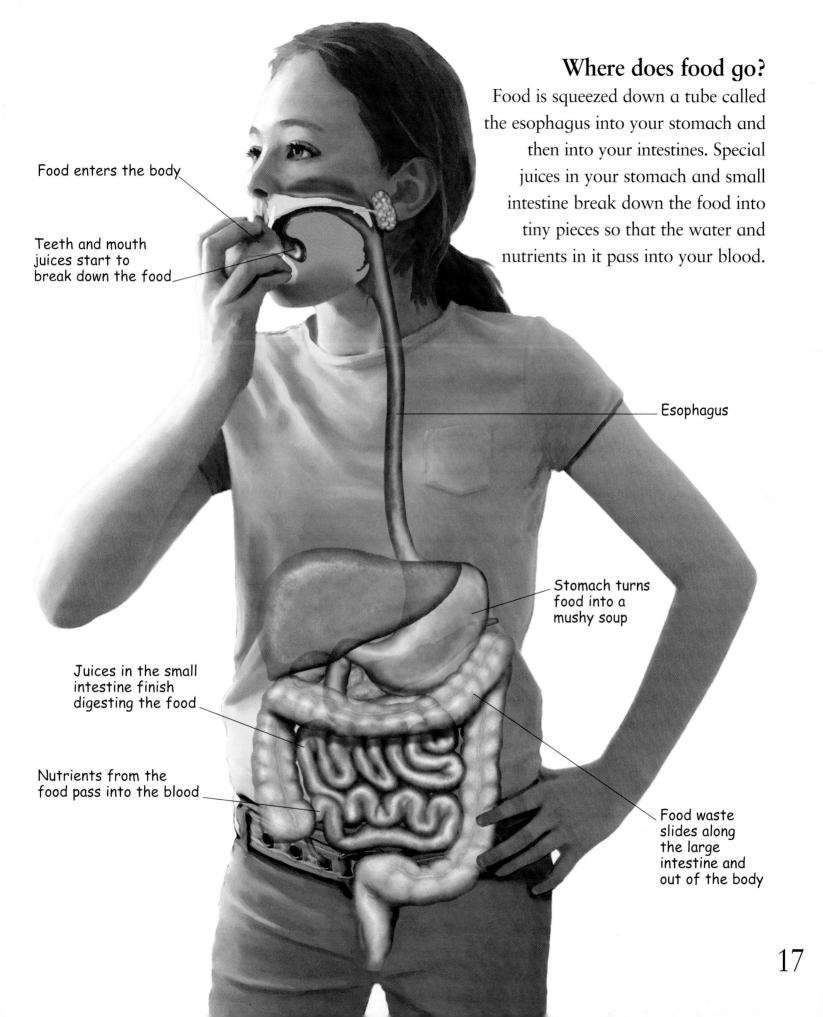

Food enters the body

Teeth and mouth juices start to break down the food

Where does food go?

Food is squeezed down a tube called the esophagus into your stomach and then into your intestines. Special juices in your stomach and small intestine break down the food into tiny pieces so that the water and nutrients in it pass into your blood.

Esophagus

Stomach turns food into a mushy soup

Juices in the small intestine finish digesting the food

Nutrients from the food pass into the blood

Food waste slides along the large intestine and out of the body

17

Breathing

You breathe because your body needs a gas called oxygen in order to stay alive. Oxygen gets into your body when you breathe in air through your nose or mouth. This air goes into your lungs, where oxygen passes into your blood. Your blood carries it all over your body.

Air tank

Scuba diver

Yawning

No one is exactly sure why you yawn. It may be that you are not breathing deeply enough and yawning gets more oxygen to your brain.

Breathing in space

In space there is no air, so astronauts take a supply of air with them. Your body cannot survive without air, even for just a few minutes.

Breathing underwater

Water contains oxygen, but we cannot breathe in water. If people want to swim underwater for a long time, they take tanks of air with them.

18

Looking at lungs

You have two lungs in your chest. They are connected to your throat by a tube called the trachea, also called the windpipe or airway. Below your lungs is a sheet of muscle called the diaphragm, which helps you breathe in and out.

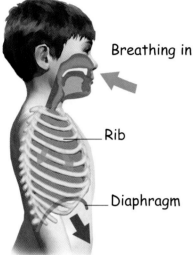

Breathing in

Rib

Diaphragm

Air is sucked into the lungs as the diaphragm flattens and the chest muscles lift the ribs up and out.

The trachea divides into two tubes, one going to each lung. There they branch into many smaller tubes.

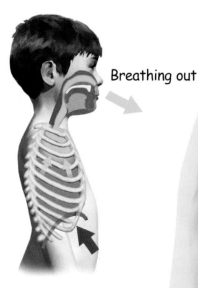

Breathing out

Air is pushed out of the lungs as the diaphragm relaxes and the ribs move in and down.

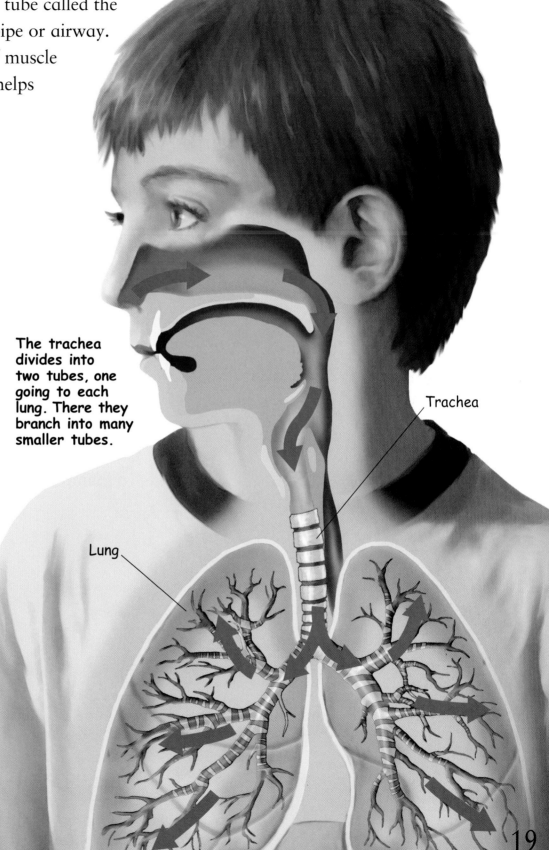

Trachea

Lung

19

Your beating heart

Your heart is a special type of muscle. It beats all the time, day and night, without you even having to think about it. Your heart beats in order to pump blood carrying nutrients and oxygen to all parts of your body and to take away wastes.

Doctors listen to the heart using a stethoscope.

Thump, thump

Your heartbeat is made by little gates in the heart called valves. These valves slam shut with a thump after blood is pumped through them.

A strong heart

Exercise keeps your heart strong. When you exercise, your heart beats harder and faster to send more blood to your muscles. The blood contains oxygen, which your muscles use in order to release energy.

A double pump

Your heart has two pumps. The right side pumps blood to the lungs, where it collects oxygen. The left side pumps the oxygen-rich blood around the body in thin tubes called blood vessels.

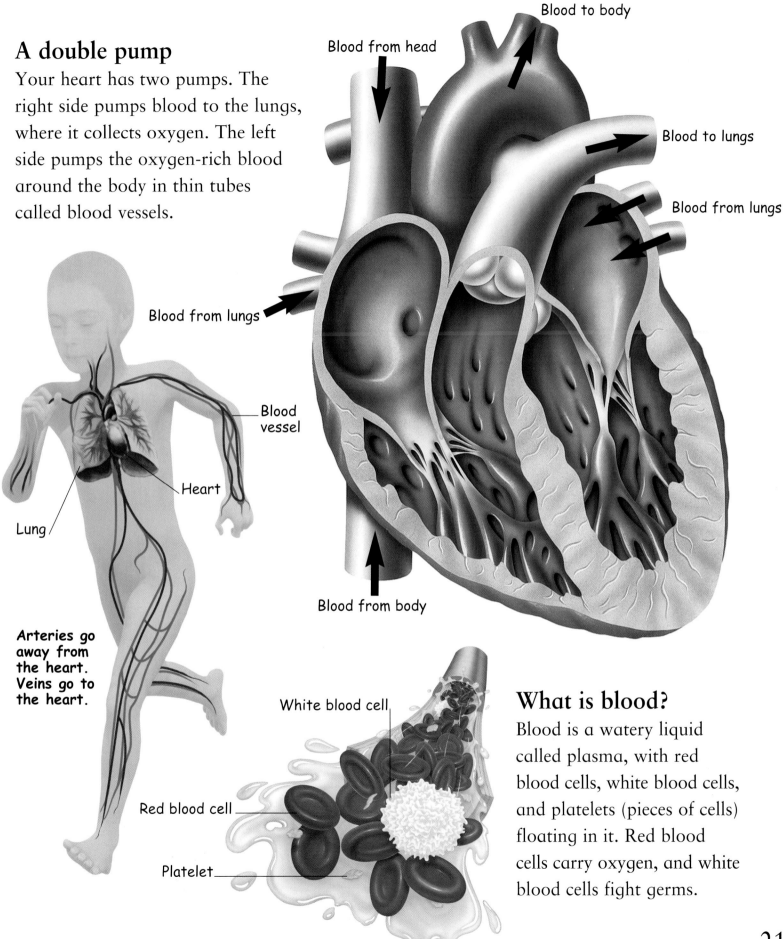

Blood from head

Blood to body

Blood to lungs

Blood from lungs

Blood from lungs

Blood from body

Blood vessel

Heart

Lung

Arteries go away from the heart. Veins go to the heart.

White blood cell

Red blood cell

Platelet

What is blood?

Blood is a watery liquid called plasma, with red blood cells, white blood cells, and platelets (pieces of cells) floating in it. Red blood cells carry oxygen, and white blood cells fight germs.

21

Your bony body

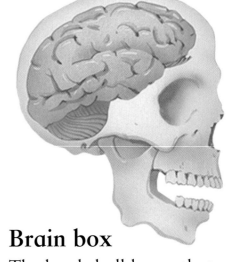

Your bony skeleton holds up your body. It also gives it its shape and protects the softer parts inside such as your heart and brain. Bones are strong and hard, but they are also alive! As you grow, they get bigger.

Brain box

The hard skull bones that you can feel on your head protect the soft, delicate brain underneath.

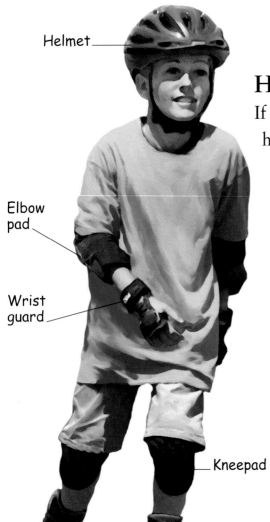

Helmet

Elbow pad

Wrist guard

Kneepad

Sometimes your body needs extra padding to help protect your bones.

Healing bones

If bones break, they usually heal themselves. Sometimes they need to be held in place in a plaster cast so that they can heal in the correct position.

X-rays of broken bones help doctors see where the break is and check how it is healing.

22

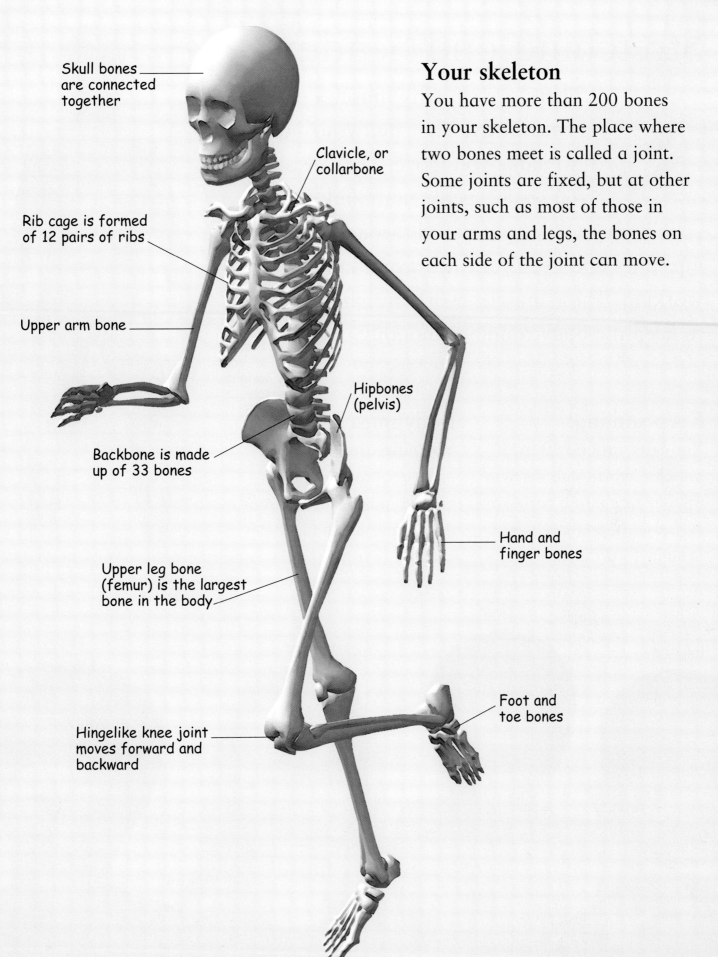

Skull bones are connected together

Clavicle, or collarbone

Rib cage is formed of 12 pairs of ribs

Upper arm bone

Hipbones (pelvis)

Backbone is made up of 33 bones

Hand and finger bones

Upper leg bone (femur) is the largest bone in the body

Foot and toe bones

Hingelike knee joint moves forward and backward

Your skeleton

You have more than 200 bones in your skeleton. The place where two bones meet is called a joint. Some joints are fixed, but at other joints, such as most of those in your arms and legs, the bones on each side of the joint can move.

Stretching and bending

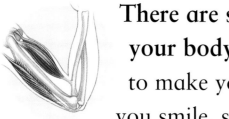

There are stretchy muscles all over your body. They pull your bones to make you move. They also help you smile, speak, and blink. Inside your body muscles push food through your intestines and keep your heart and lungs working. These muscles work automatically to keep the body running smoothly.

More than one third of your body weight is muscle.

Keep smiling!

You have around 30 face muscles, which pull the skin of your face into a variety of expressions. Smiling uses around 15 different muscles.

Body muscles

You have around 650 muscles in total. Your biggest muscles are in your thighs and bottom. The smallest is in your ear!

Excited

Tired

Sad

Happy

Bendable body

When you do a backbend, your brain sends a signal to tell the correct muscles to get shorter. Doing this takes a lot of energy, which your muscles mostly get from sugars in the blood.

Biceps muscle

Triceps muscle

In order to raise your arm, the biceps gets shorter and fatter and the triceps relaxes and stretches. To lower your arm, the opposite happens.

Working in pairs

Most muscles work in pairs because they can only make themselves shorter. They need another muscle pulling the other way to make them stretch out again.

Building muscles

If you do a lot of exercise, your muscles get stronger. People who lose strength or movement in one part of their body can often make up for it by using another part, like this cyclist using her arms for power.

Hands and feet

Did you know that around half of your body's bones are in your hands and feet? You have 27 bones in each hand and 26 bones in each foot. There are also around 20 muscles in each hand and foot. Your feet are like flexible platforms for your body, while your hands allow you to grip and hold things, as well as to feel them with your fingertips.

Tendon

Flexible fingers

Your thumb can touch each one of your fingertips. This allows you to hold small objects such as needles or flower stems.

Wrist ropes

Ropelike tendons run from your wrist to your fingertips, connecting them to your hand and arm muscles, which control most finger movements.

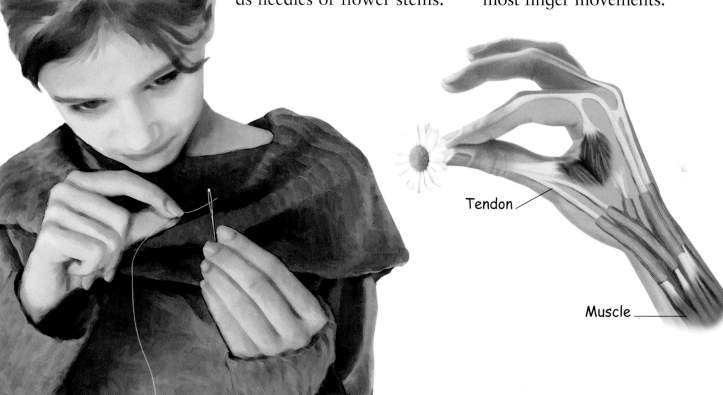

Tendon

Muscle

Foot belt

The straplike belt around the foot holds the muscles and tendons close to the bones that they pull. Can you see a similar band around the picture of the wrist on page 26?

Springy sole

The bottom of your foot gives a spring to your step when you walk or run. The curved shape of the foot's arch helps spread your body's weight over your heel and toes as you walk or stand.

Toes are shorter and less flexible than fingers.

Fingernail

Bone

Nails protect the tips of your fingers and toes. It takes around six months to grow a new fingernail.

Few animals can walk and run on two legs. Being able to do this is useful because it leaves your hands free for other tasks.

27

Growing up

You began your life inside of your mother's abdomen. There you grew and developed for around nine months until you were ready to be born. When you were a baby, you had to be taken care of all the time. Gradually, you learned how to take care of yourself, as well as more difficult skills such as talking and reading.

A baby begins

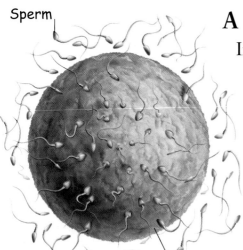

Sperm

Egg

If a sperm from a man joins with an egg cell inside of a woman, a baby starts to grow. Out of all of the sperm in this picture, only one will join with the egg.

Baby bag

Inside of your mother you floated around inside of a bag full of liquid, which kept you safe from knocks and bumps. You got all your food and air from your mother until you were ready to be born.

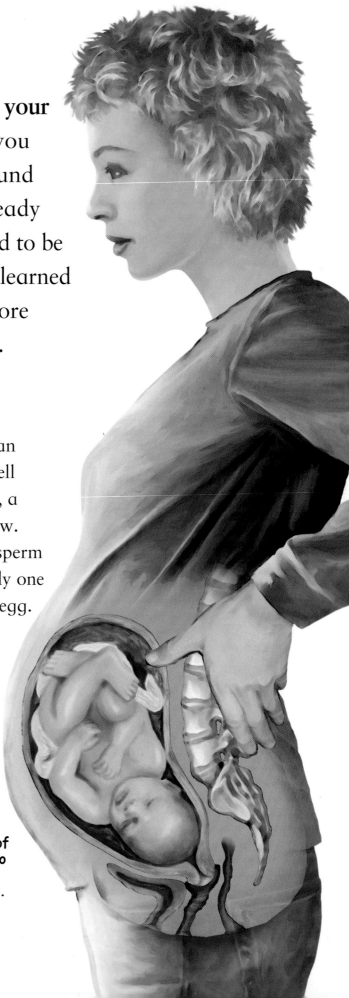

When babies are ready to be born, they usually turn around inside of their mother so that they are born headfirst.

28

A newborn baby cannot control its muscles very well, so it cannot stand or move around very much.

Learning new skills

A newborn baby's muscles are weak, and it can't even hold up its head. But by the time it is around one year old, it has learned to crawl, walk, and probably say a few words.

Babies have a good sense of taste. They also learn how things feel by putting them into their mouth.

In order to ride a bike, your brain has to control the way you see, balance, and move—all at the same time!

Between the ages of 9 and 12 months, a baby starts to crawl and explore its surroundings.

Around the time of a baby's first birthday, it takes its first steps.

Staying healthy

In order to stay healthy, you need many different types of food and plenty of water. It is also important to keep your body clean, exercise regularly, and get enough rest and sleep. A clean, healthy body has a better chance of fighting off germs and diseases.

Exercise keeps your body flexible and strong. Exercise also makes your heart and lungs work hard, which helps them stay in good condition.

Brushing your teeth

It is a good idea to brush your teeth at least twice a day. If you don't, bacteria feed on pieces of leftover food and produce acids, which make holes in your teeth and can give you a toothache.

Glossary

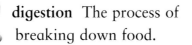

abdomen The lower half of the main part of your body (your trunk), between your chest and your legs.

arteries Thick-walled tubes that carry blood from your heart to other parts of your body. This blood usually contains a lot of oxygen.

bacteria Single-celled living things that can only be seen with a microscope.

bladder A stretchy bag in your abdomen that collects liquid wastes (urine).

blood vessels Tubes that carry blood all over your body.

cells The tiny living units that make up your body.

dentin A tough substance in your teeth, below the enamel.

diaphragm A dome-shaped muscle, used in breathing.

digestion The process of breaking down food.

enamel A very hard substance that coats your teeth.

iris The colored part of your eye.

joint The place where two bones meet.

melanin The brown coloring that gives skin, hair, and eyes some of their color and helps protect the skin from sunlight.

nerves Wirelike threads in your body that carry electrical messages to and from your brain and the rest of your body.

organs Parts of the body, such as the heart and lungs, that perform different tasks.

oxygen A gas in the air. You need to breathe oxygen in order to stay alive and release energy from your food.

plasma The watery liquid that carries your blood cells and contains dissolved substances such as salts.

platelets Tiny fragments of cells in your blood that help it clot.

protein A substance in food that helps your body grow and repair itself.

pupil An opening in your iris where light enters your eye.

skeleton A strong framework of bones that supports and protects your body and helps you move.

tendons Strong threads that connect muscles to bones.

trachea The main air tube, or windpipe, that goes from the back of your throat to your lungs.

trunk The middle section of your body.

veins Thin-walled tubes that carry blood back to your heart. This blood does not usually contain much oxygen.

vocal cords Two flaps in your throat that vibrate when air from your lungs passes over them.

Index